Back to Basics

ENGLISH

for 5-6 year olds

BOOK ONE

Sheila Lane and Marion Kemp

a b c

a is for ant

apple

axe   alligator

a a a a a a

a a a a a a

b is for **bed**

balloon   ball

b   b   b   b   b   b

c is for **car**

cat   clock

c c c c

c c c c c

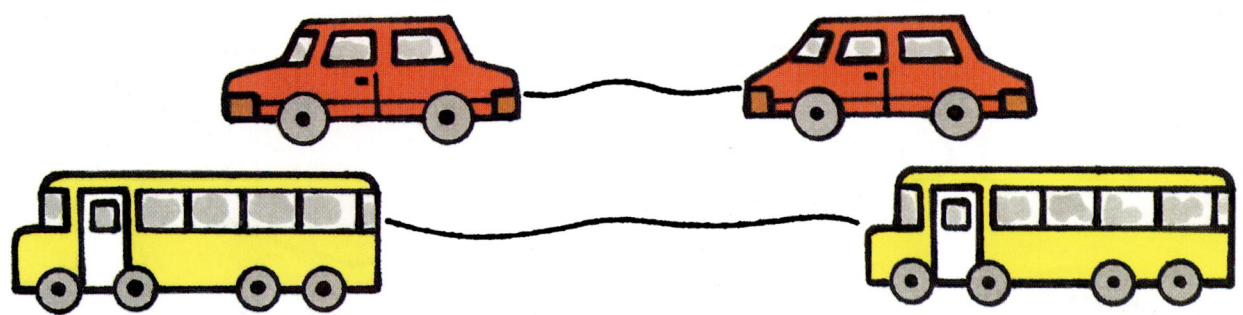

Match the pictures.

ant   cat   bat   ant

Match the words and pictures.

cow   bee   cow   ape

ape   cow   bee   ape

bee   ape   cow   bee

a b c   d e f

d is for dish

drum

dog

dinosaur

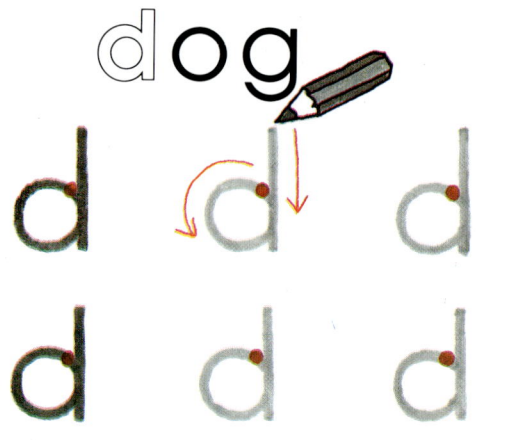

e is for egg

egg-cup   elephant

e e e e e e e

f is for flag

fish

face

f f f f f f f
f f f f f f f

Match the sounds and pictures.

Make funny faces.

d e f g h i

g is for glove

girl

gate

go

g g g g g g
g g g g g g

h is for hand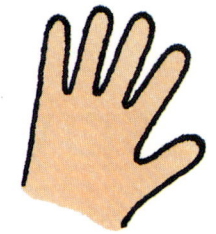

house hat

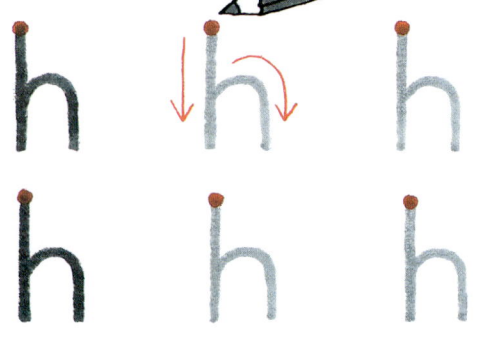
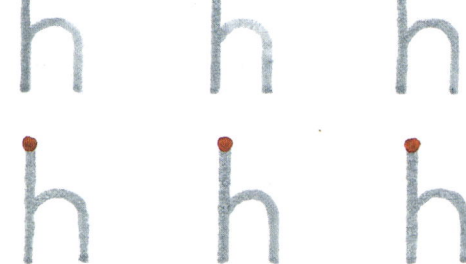

i is for ivy

ice-cream insect

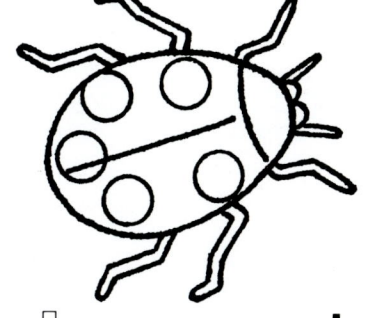

 spy . . . h

Which toys begin with h?

TOY SHOP

homes

Where do they live?

g h i j k l m

j is for jug

jack-in-the-box

j j j j j j j

k is for king

kite

k k k k k k k

14

l is for lolly

leaf   lion

l l l l l l

m is for mouse

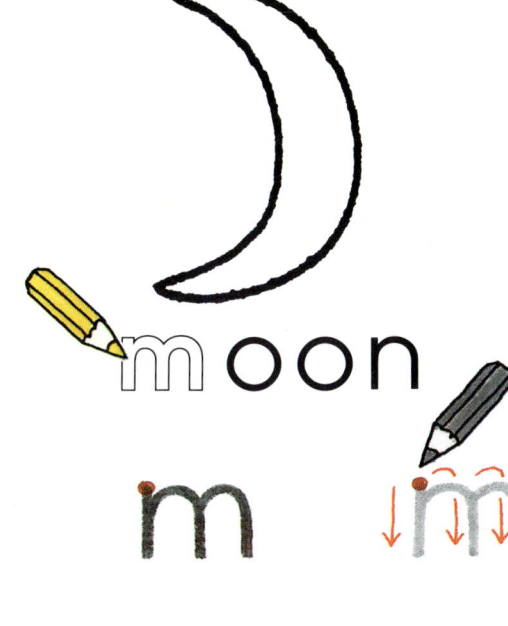 

moon   man

m m m m m

m m m m m

2 by 2

Match the animals.

2 cats

2 monkeys

2 goats

2 lions

1 2 3 4 5
one two three four five

three

Match the words and pictures.

one

three

five

four

two

a mouse in a house

two cats in a hat

j k l m n o p q

n is for nest

nose　　　　　net

n n n n n n n

o is for octopus

orange　　　owl

o o o o o o o

p is for pig

pear pencil

p p p p p p p

q is for quack

I can quack!

queen

q q q q q q q
q q q q q q q

Look

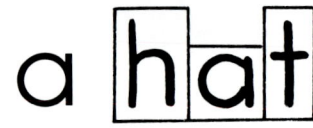 a hat    a pig

Write over the letters.

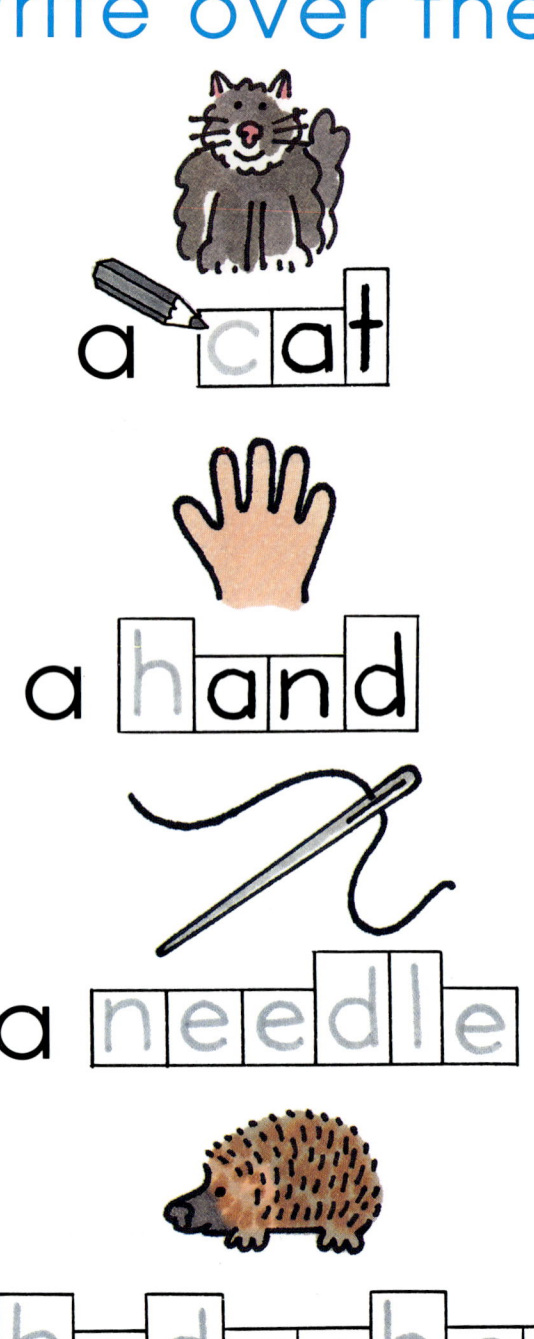

a cat

a hand

a needle

a bag

a flag

a lamp

 a 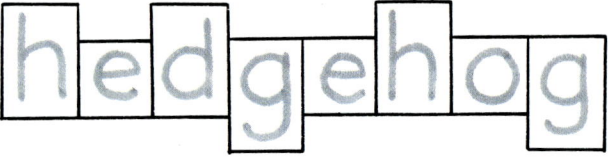 hedgehog   a 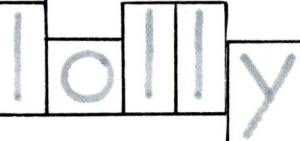 lolly

a horse in
a house

Write over the words.

a beetle in
a bed

a man in
the moon

n o p q r s t

r is for rocket

rainbow rabbit

r r r r r r

s is for star

sausages snowman

s s s s s s

t is for table

tree tortoise

tomato tiger

1	**2**	**3**	**4**
one	two	three	four

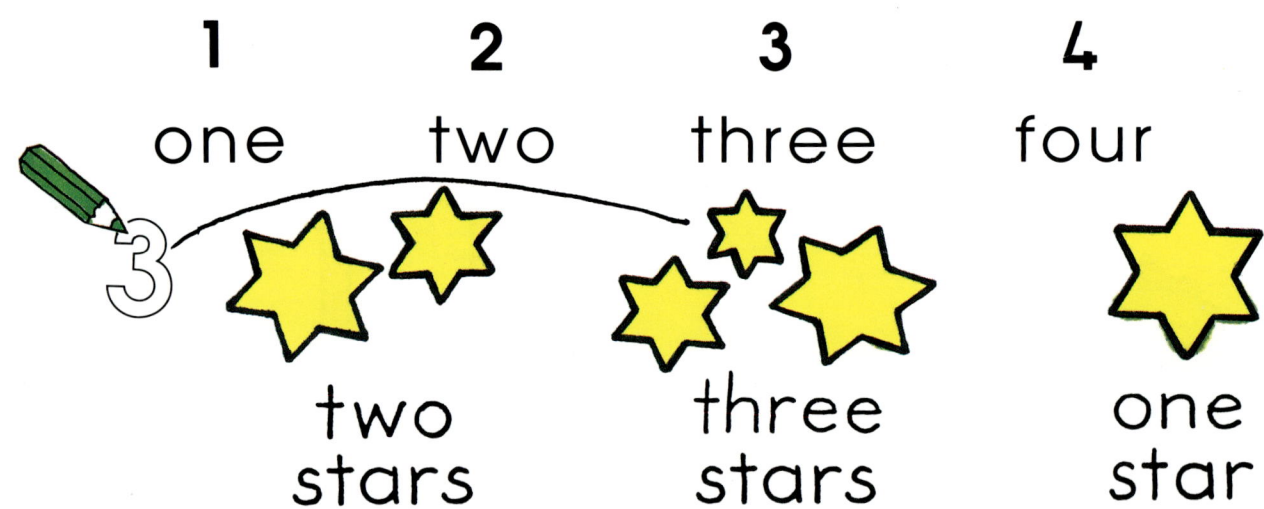

two stars	three stars	one star

Match the number.

4

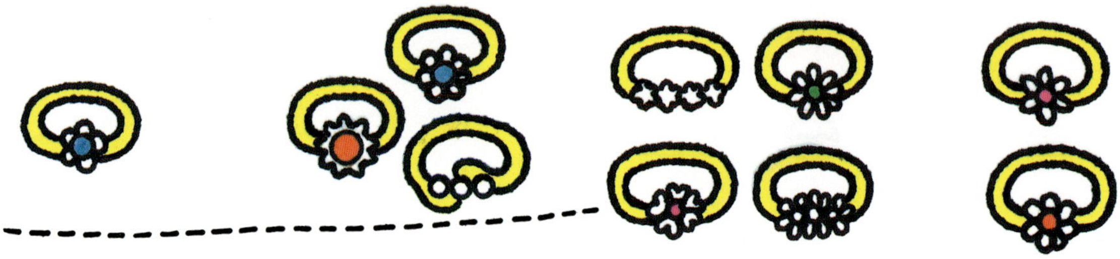

one ring	three rings	four rings	two rings

1

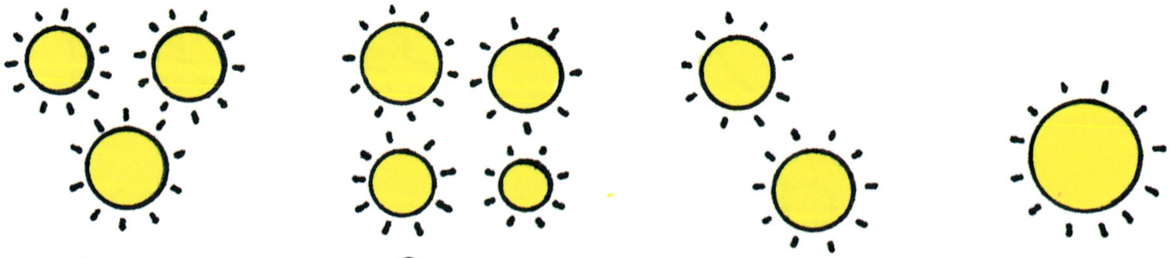

three suns	four suns	two suns	one sun

2

four swans	two swans	one swan	three swans

I spy ... t

tank trumpet train

tortoise top tiger

r s t   u v w

u is for
umbrella

u is for up

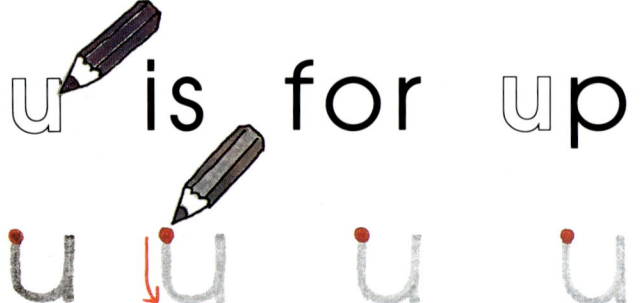

a rainbow
up in the sky

two kites
in the sky

v is for van

v vests

v v v v v v v

w is for window

w all

w w w w w

Which words begin with w?

Humpty Dumpty sat on a wall

vest		watch
window	man	queen
vase	umbrella	whale
van	witch	rainbow

u v w x y z

x is for x-ray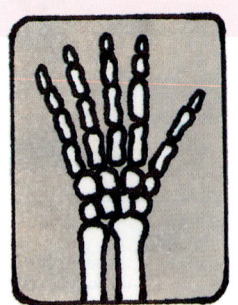

xylophone

x x x x x x

y is for yellow

yoghurt

y y y y y y

z is for zebra

zip   zigzag

z z z z z z z

z is for zoo

penguins giraffes
ZOO
zebras polar bears

Colour the words on the big card to match the words on the small cards.

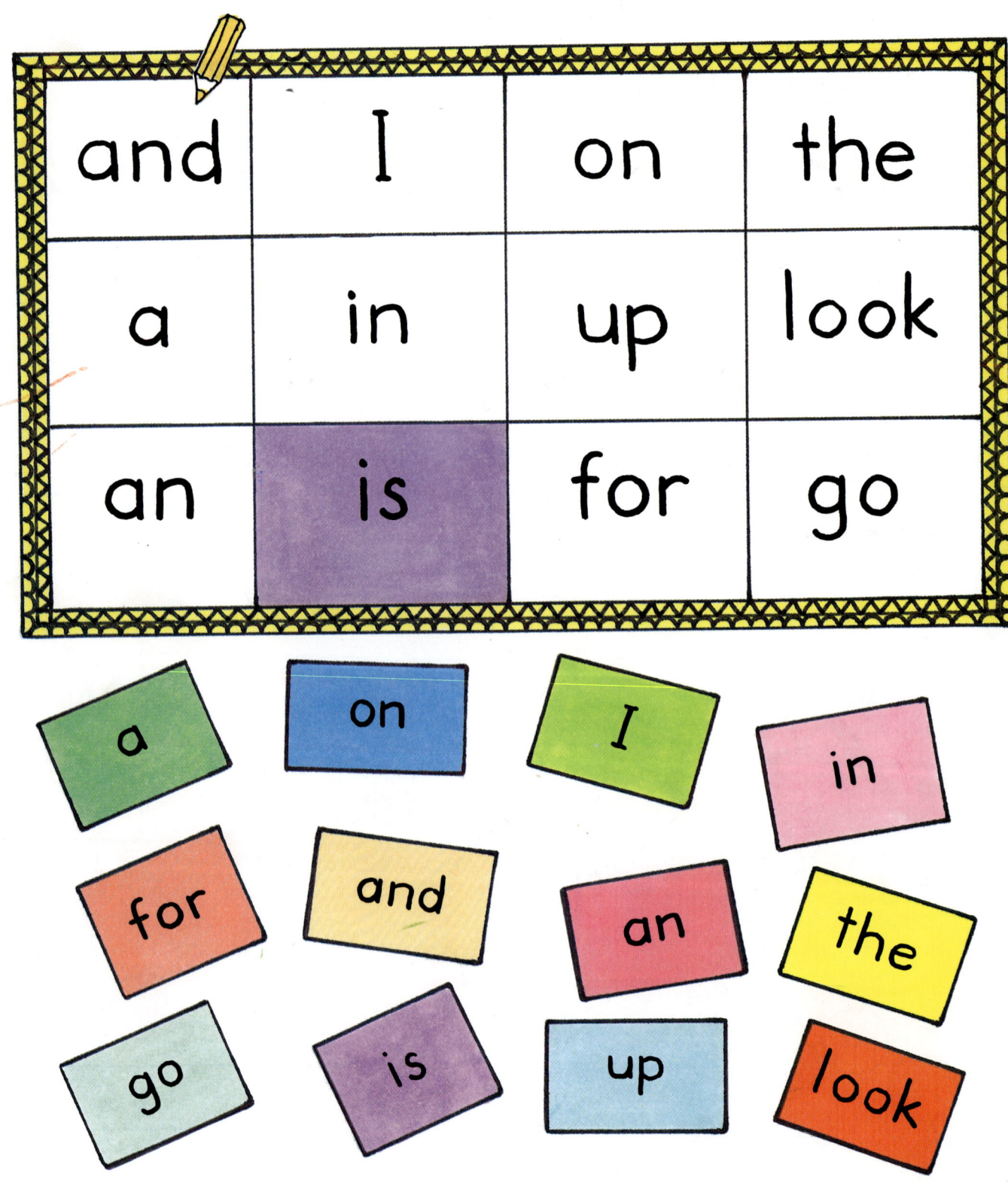